REDDY GET READY

A Seussian Worm (Tail) Tale

by

Anna Goodwin MS &

Ronald Goodwin PHD

Illustrations by

Josephie Dean Jackson

I

Reddy Get Ready
A Seussian Worm (Tail) Tale

Text Copyright © 2018 by Anna Goodwin
Illustration Copyright © 2018 by Josephie Dean Jackson

All rights reserved. No part of this book may be reproduced or transmitted in any form or by any means without written permission of the publisher.

ISBN: ebook: 978-1-940025-41-4
         print: 978-1-940025-36-0

Library of Congress Control Number: 2018908974

1. Worms-children's fiction-Seussian Tale. 2. Earthworms-value-fiction. 3. earthworms-scientific facts. 4. Earthworms-science education. 5. earthworms-how to grow. I. Title

Designed by:
Jera Publishing

Published by:
Bitterroot Mountain Publishing House LLC
4319 Echo Glenn Lane
Coeur d'Alene, ID 83815
www.bmphmedia.com

Bitterroot Mountain
PUBLISHING

10 9 8 7 6 5 4 3 2 1

Printed in the United States of America.

For our dearest grandchildren

Mei, Shana, and Carter from Oma and Opa

Anna and Ronald Goodwin

For my darling Pippa,

"No mud, no lotus." Thich Nhet Hanh

"Shhh, Mommy, listen to the ants working."

2 year old Pippa

So glad you were born.

Love Mommy.

Josephie Dean Jackson

CONTENTS

Dear Parents, Home School Parents, and Teachers,

Have the children learn facts about earthworms and why they are so important to us all.

Create a worm bin at home or at school and have the children feed and watch the worms create fertilizer for our precious earth.

Last of all do a research experiment with them.

Have fun, and learn!

This is a story of Reddy the red worm and his invaluable contributions to our world even though he is tiny and thinks he is useless. My husband, Ronald H. Goodwin PHD, (a research entomologist for the USDA and an ecologist for most of his life) and I (a psychotherapist, writer, and associate professor) created this story originally for our grandchildren, with the assistance of our son Jason, our daughter Tonya, and son-in-law Chris.

We combined psychology and the ecology of the earth to help children learn about the environment as well as how important each one of them is, just like Reddy, even though they are small and often feel they have no worth. Ron and I grew red worms for several years both for our home garden use as well as for sale to local adventurers like us. We hope that you and your children will learn as much and enjoy this venture as much as we did.

My husband passed away a couple of years ago and he would be honored to know that children from every corner of the world could benefit from his great passion, his work, and his contribution to this precious world. More than anything besides his family, Ron loved nature. Keep our earth safe and in loving hands.

The illustrator Josephie Dean Jackson, is originally from Australia, is a tea farmer and the CEO of several start-up companies in America. She has been drawing, sculpting, creating and painting since she can remember. Her daughter's French bulldog, Frank (@lifebyfrank), was the inspiration for Reddy's expressions. She encourages children and adults alike to explore the natural sciences and "Please, please learn the differences between bees and wasps!"

Take good care of yourselves and your children,

Anna

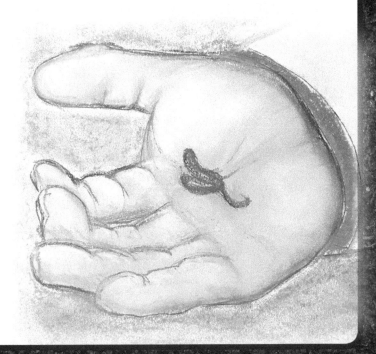

Reddy the red worm curled up in dismay.

His Papa was coming to take him away.

"Tomorrow we move," he had heard Papa say.

Tomorrow had come and today was the day.

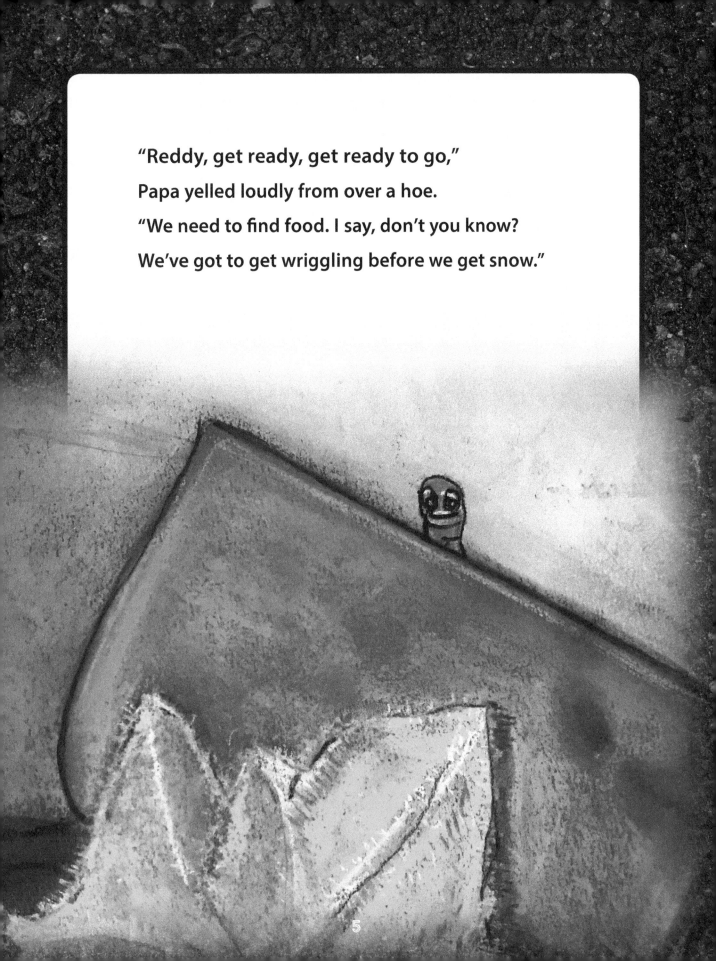

"Reddy, get ready, get ready to go,"
Papa yelled loudly from over a hoe.
"We need to find food. I say, don't you know?
We've got to get wriggling before we get snow."

Wee Reddy McGee peaked out from his ball.

He could hear Mama counting from up on the wall.

Thirty-six brothers and sisters in all

Lined up on a dirt pile from tiny to tall.

As Reddy McGee got ready to go

He saw a large bee buzz over quite low

And land right beside him, and oh heavens no,

She polished the fur on her belly just so.

Then raising her head she glowered at him,
Her many small eyes glistened hard round the rim.
"Yuck worms," she said. "Ugly, so slimy and slim.
Not even a hair, not even a limb."

She shook her small leg at him,

showed off her fuzz

Then hovered right over and gave him a buzz.

"At least I make honey and that's just because.

You're good for nothing. You're just a scuzz."

"Papa," asked Reddy, "Am I of no worth?
Should I have been born a bee on this earth?
Is there nothing at all I've done since my birth
Except maybe add on a bit to my girth?"

Then Papa swished back his tail in a huff.
"Don't worry your head with that sort of stuff.
Who cares if bees think you're not good enough.
I love you all without hair, fur, or fluff."

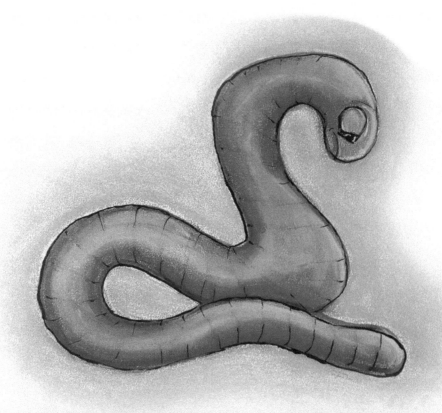

But Reddy McGee wasn't certain at all.

That bee might be right. Was he ugly and small?

Besides he was useless, no good at all.

All he did was eat and tunnel holes at a crawl.

The worm family wriggled and dug through the night.

By daybreak his Papa looked tired and uptight.

But Reddy kept digging with all of his might

He knew he'd find food if he did it just right.

All of a sudden small Reddy McGee

Burst through the earth holding up a green pea.

Papa sniffed and he sniffed, then shouted with glee,

"A food pile! You've done it, my Reddy McGee."

They slurped and they burped the juice of a melon.

The mush dribbled out by almost a gallon.

Little Willie was smilin' and Pippin was yellin'

"One more sip and I'll burst," sighed big sister Helen.

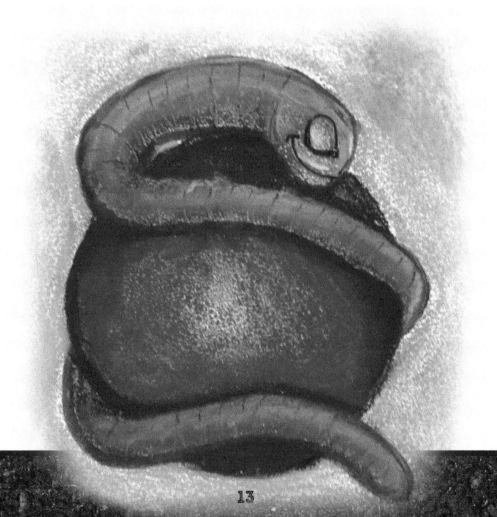

Mama yawned wide and looked up at the sky.
The sun had come up and was riding quite high.
"Humans and birds will come. Oh me, oh my.
We got to get moving or we may all die."

Papa dove deep and led them to bed.

"Now don't you forget, stay here," Mama said.

Each worm, except Reddy, nodded a head.

But Reddy McGee got ready instead.

He waited till Papa gave out a loud snore

And tunneled his way to the surface once more.

He had to find out what he was good for,

Or if he was rotten, right down to the core.

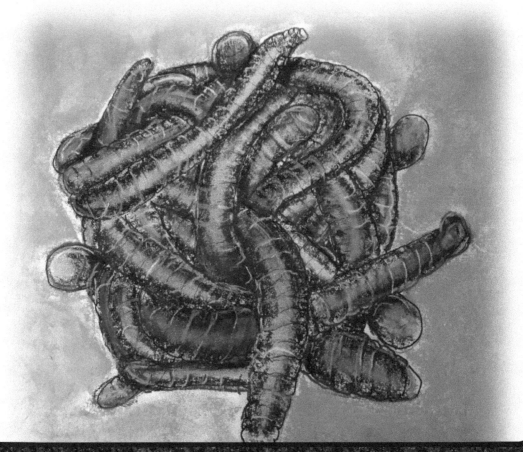

He poked out his head and tried not to blink.

When a big yellow eye just gave him a wink.

Then another bird came with a beak dark as ink

And Reddy McGee tried hard not to think.

He trembled and shook and tried to be bold,

But all of a sudden he felt very cold.

Birds would eat you alive, at least so he was told.

"You should have stayed home,"

he could hear Mama scold.

Then Reddy McGee got ready to go.

With a slap of his tail he burrowed down low.

He waited and listened and heard from below

The shriek of the black bird,

"You're much too slow."

The other bird squawked, "Now Blacky my tot.

He's not half a mouthful. Not more than a dot."

Reddy shivered and shrank and curled in a knot.

He was not even bird food.

Not worth getting got.

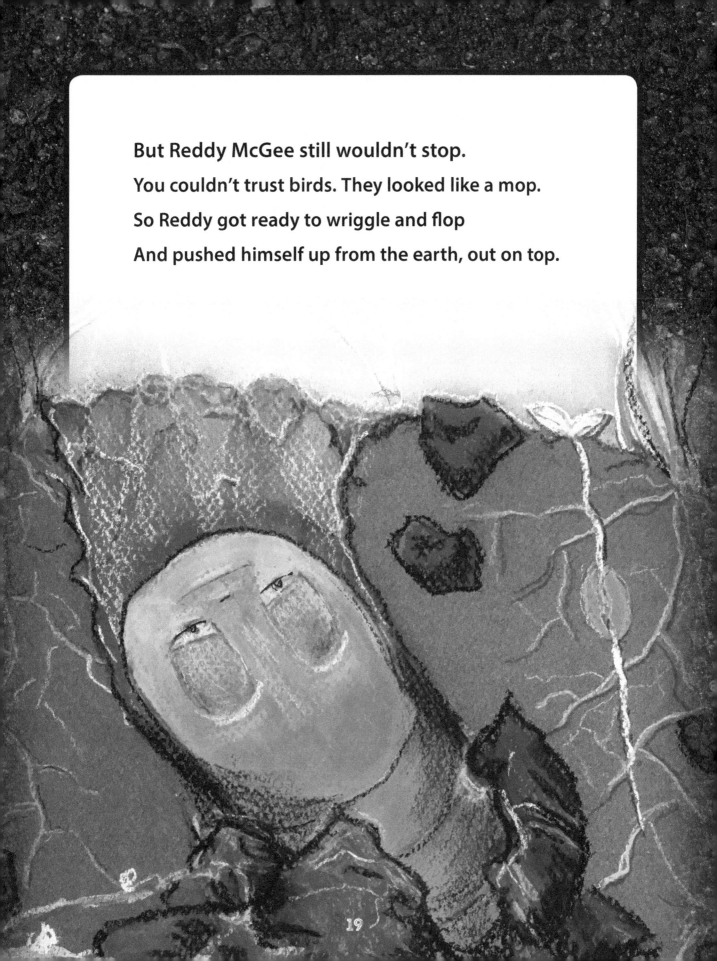

But Reddy McGee still wouldn't stop.

You couldn't trust birds. They looked like a mop.

So Reddy got ready to wriggle and flop

And pushed himself up from the earth, out on top.

He heard a loud whoosh. The birds took
to the sky.
A giant dark shadow loomed over nearby.
A new someone, somebody scooped him up high
And peered at him close with one shiny eye.

"Mother. A worm," yelled a voice with a hat.

"What should I do? Should I squash the worm flat?"

Reddy wriggled and squirmed this way and that.

His life would be over with just a small splat.

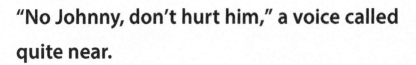

"No Johnny, don't hurt him," a voice called
quite near.

"I've been waiting and waiting for him to appear.

We can't live without him. Please bring him here."

Reddy stopped squirming and perked up his ear.

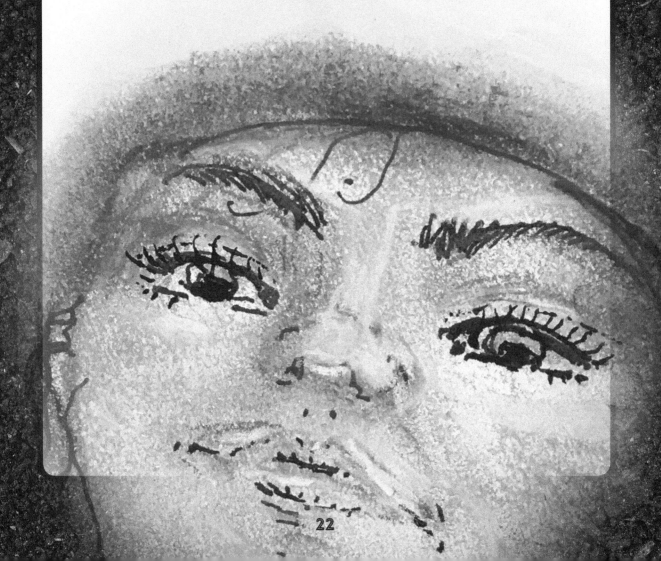

What did the human mean? He couldn't see.

Was he really important although he was wee?

But the human was silent, as silent could be.

She handled him gently and then set him free.

Now Reddy McGee had nowhere to roam.

He wriggled away. It was time to go home.

And that might have well been the end of our poem.

But suddenly plunk, he fell into some foam.

With a shake of his head the foam
whirled around.

Near him lay bubbling old fruit big and round

And many small creatures danced on the ground.

A millipede beckoned to him from a mound.

"Madame Mill Botsky,
Mill Botsky's the name.
Telling your fortune
is part of my game.
I gaze into foam balls.
That's how I got fame.
I tell you, I tell you,
I am what I claim.

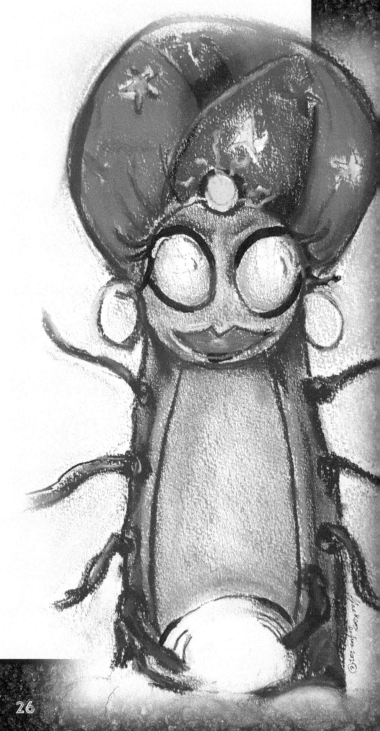

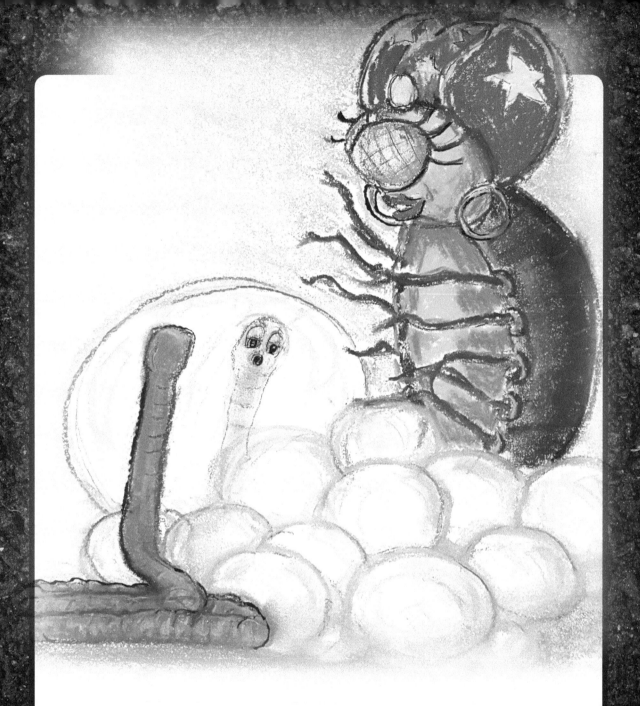

"I can tell you your future and even your past.

I can tell you why red worms value is vast.

I tell you for certain your troubles won't last

If you look in this bubble. Come over here fast."

Then Reddy McGee squirmed up on the double

And next to Mill Botsky gazed in the bubble.

With a twitch of ten legs she showed him the trouble

And all he could see was a desert with stubble.

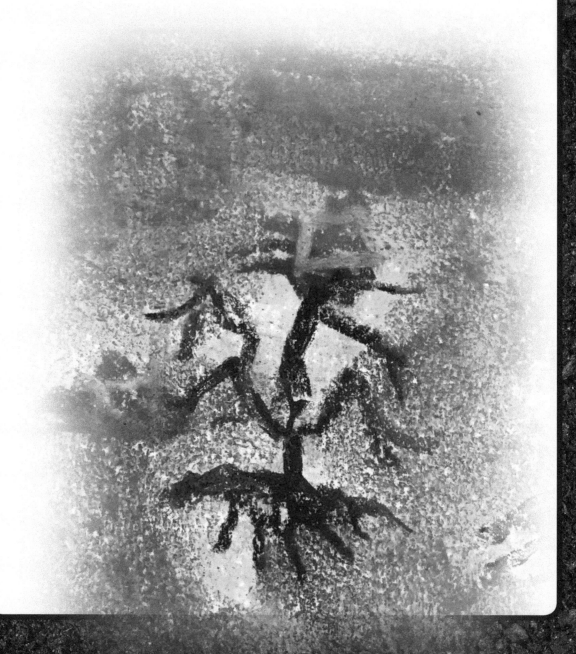

Slowly but surely he heard a low hum.

Out of the earth he could see creatures come.

Worms, ants, and saw bugs,

the mites were just some.

A cricket played fiddle,

the beetle a drum.

All kinds of small creatures dug holes all around

And brought microbes and water and air to the ground.

They chewed and they nibbled

and left a small mound,

And turned that old stubble to

more than they'd found.

With a rumble and twist
plants popped up everywhere
And Reddy McGee could
do nothing but stare.
"Without you and small
creatures the earth would be bare.
The plants couldn't grow," he heard her declare.

"Your bodies make poop that makes food for the earth.

Then you bring lots of air to help seeds give birth.

Now you know who you are. You know what you're worth.

Come meet your new friends. Come join in the mirth."

Reddy got ready and danced 'round with glee,

He bounced up a bubble and shouted, "I see.

The world is much better with me being me

And you being you and a bee that's a bee."

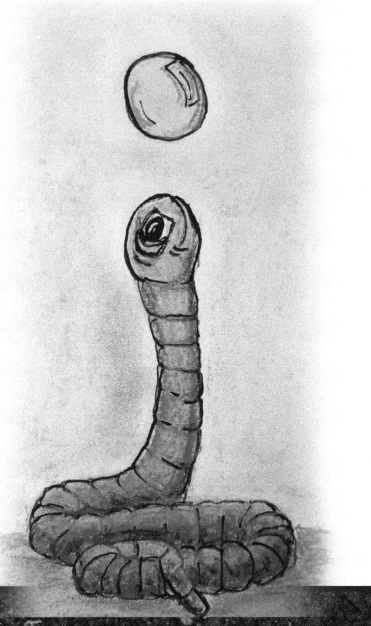

Soon Reddy was tired. He yawned and he said,

"If Mama wakes up, she'll get redder than red."

So he waved and he clapped his tail to his head.

"Let's all be ourselves." Then he crawled home to bed.

RED WORM FACTS

1. Red worms are 1 out of about 2,700 different kinds of earthworms in the world.

2. Red worm bodies have 95 segments. An earthworm has five arches/hearts that are segmented and pump blood throughout its body.

3. Red worms have no bones. They move with their muscles.

4. They have no eyes, but can sense light and dark. They prefer dark.

5. They have no ears but they can sense vibrations in the ground. They sense touch through their tiny bristles.

6. They don't have lungs. They breathe through their moist skin and have red blood. This is why it is very important for their skin to stay moist.

7. Their head is a little bigger than their tail and they use it like a shovel to move earth.

8. Red worms have an organ called a ganglia, which is similar to a very small brain.

9. The worms hatch from a cocoon in 3 weeks. It takes 6 weeks till they are grown and they live from 1 to 2 years. The population can double in 90 days.

10. They eat their body weight in food each day.

11. There are usually more than a million earthworms in an acre of land.

12. They can burrow down over 6 feet in the soil.

13. They make a secret slime on their body with nitrogen in it. It helps them move their bodies through the dirt.

14. They are neither male or female but both.

15. The strangest fact is that as long as the head is intact it can often re-grow injured parts of the body.

*Parents or teachers, have the children read the worm facts after they read the story. Then have them pick out the aspects of the story that are not factual. (e.g. worms don't have ears and can't hear.) See how many they can find.

WHY ARE WORMS SO IMPORTANT TO OUR EARTH?

1. They dig holes in the earth and mix air with the soil and loosen it. These little tunnels also allow water to filter easily into the soil so the plants can grow.

2. They break down the plants they eat with the enzymes and microbes in their gut.

3. Their poop (castings) is full of nutrients and bacteria along with plant growth hormones and humic acid that improve plant growth. Their poop is used as fertilizer both in this country and developing countries.

4. Red worms are usually a growers choice to rear because they create the most fertilizer for the amount of food they eat.

GROW YOUR OWN RED WORMS

MAKE A COMPOSTING BIN.

1. Go online to find a good place to buy 1 or 2 lbs. of red worms. Make sure you request red worms not just earthworms. Red worms are much more efficient composters than other worms. The worms will be sent priority mail.

2. Prepare a bin before they arrive. Buy a plastic bin about 16" x 24" x 8" at any hardware or grocery store. Wash it well and place it on a plastic pan. Drill tiny holes in the lower sides to allow the worm liquid to flow out onto the pan. The dark liquid is great fertilizer water to pour on your plants.

3. Prepare the bedding. Tear or shred a newspaper or two into about 1" strips (no colored paper). Dampen the paper but don't make it soggy. Place the paper into the bin keeping the paper fluffy so the bin is about 3/4 full. The worms will eat the paper.

4. Sprinkle 2-4 cups of ordinary soil over the paper. The soil helps the worms digestion and provides microbes.

5. When the worms arrive, place them gently into the prepared bin.

6. Feed the worms leftover fruits and vegetables (No meats, bones, oils, or dairy products and limited citrus fruits). By the way, they love watermelon and ground coffee remains. Cut up fruits and vegetables into small pieces or shred. Bury the food in the bin. For a pound of worms add about 3 pounds of food per week. Feed a couple of times a week. Have the children place their leftovers on top and watch the worms feed.

7. Cover the bedding with sheets of dry newspaper to keep in the moisture. If bedding dries up spray it with water or if too wet add dry shredded newspaper.

8. Loosely cover the bin with the lid but leave it ajar to allow in air. Fluff up bedding weekly to make sure the worms are getting enough air.

9. Place the bin away from windows, heating, and air-conditioning in a place that remains between 55 and 75 degrees. They can't survive in cold or heat. In nature they would burrow deeply into the soil to keep their environment constant.

10. Don't be grossed out by the liquid coming off the compost. It is quite valuable and called "Worm Tea" or "Compost Tea". Make sure you empty the tray underneath the bin and check it often so it does not overflow. This makes for amazing fertilizer for your plants too.

RESEARCH STUDY TO CONDUCT WITH YOUR CHILDREN

1. Get two small, equal sized plastic pots with holes in the bottom and place on a saucer.

2. Fill one pot with ordinary soil (not fertilized soil).

3. After 6 months of feeding the worms, mix the worm soil and take an equal amount of worm soil from the bin. Place it into the second pot.

4. Get two same kind, equal size plants and plant them into the pots.

5. Water with same water (no fertilizer), equal amounts at same time, as needed.

6. Place plants side by side in the same window or same place outside.

7. Watch the plants grow and see which plant grows faster and larger.

8. Discuss the findings with your children.

CPSIA information can be obtained
at www.ICGtesting.com
Printed in the USA
JSHW011146191119
2535JS00001B/2